Original title:
In the Vine's Shadow

Copyright © 2025 Creative Arts Management OÜ
All rights reserved.

Author: Evelyn Hartman
ISBN HARDBACK: 978-1-80567-039-1
ISBN PAPERBACK: 978-1-80567-119-0

Sanctuary of Sipping Secrets

In a corner where grapes unwind,
Secret whispers leave you blind.
Wobbly chairs and chatter so sweet,
Pour a glass and plant your feet.

Laughter bounces off the wall,
Tipsy tales both large and small.
Spill your drink, it's just the start,
In this nook, we share our heart.

Gloriously Green Reveries

Grapes are rolling down the lane,
Plant a dream, it grows insane.
Will the wine cure all our woes?
Or just paint our noses rose?

Leaves are dancing with delight,
As we swig beneath the light.
A hiccup here, a snort or two,
In this green, all's fresh and new.

Tranquil Truths from Buried Roots

Digging deep where secrets lie,
You might find a cheeky pie.
Roots take hold, while we just grin,
What a world, let the fun begin!

Unearthing laughter underground,
Each sip brings a joyful sound.
A mystery wrapped in a cork,
We toast to life, and then we gawk.

Revelations of the Wine-laden Wind

The breeze whispers tales so fine,
Of grapes that wear a coat of wine.
A gust of fun, a splash of cheer,
Come raise your glass, let's persevere!

In the air, mischief does swirl,
As laughter and giggles unfurl.
With every sip, our worries lift,
Cheers to the wind, our sweetest gift!

Enclaves of Enchantment

Beneath the leaves, the grapes all squeak,
They giggle and wiggle, quite the cheek.
The sun above gives them a laugh,
While squirrels plot their fruity gaff.

A little raccoon steals a sip,
With sticky paws, he takes a trip.
Together they dance under bright skies,
In this secret world where joy never dies.

The Scent of Lost Harvests

Ants march forth with tiny drums,
They've found the stash of snacking crumbs.
With every bite, they let out cheers,
While the grapes roll and mock their fears.

A fox in a hat claims, "This is mine!"
While doves argue about the best wine.
Nature's mess becomes a grand feast,
As laughter floats from the greatest beast.

Beneath Nature's Gilded Canopy

Beneath the trees, the critters plot,
A party's brewing, but don't get caught!
The raccoons bring out the old punch bowl,
While fireflies sip and twinkle their goals.

As shadows dance in a blurry twist,
They share grape jokes that can't be missed.
Wisdom from owls? It's all a prank,
As nature laughs, all her creatures rank.

When Shadows Meet the Harvest Moon

Under the moon, all the shadows play,
With squeaks and snaps, they join the fray.
Grapes roll along, wearing tiny hats,
Eating cheese with rather chubby rats.

The night gets wild with giggles and cheers,
While owls chuckle, sharing old beers.
In this funny frenzy, songs fill the air,
Where laughter's the harvest, in every scare.

Whispers of the Grape

In a vineyard, grapes do chat,
Sharing secrets, where pests are at.
"I spilled my juice!" one tragic tale,
"My wrinkly skin? A grape gone pale!"

The sun above, it shines so bright,
While grapes complain, just out of sight.
"This juice is sweet, but who can tell,
With that ugly bug? Oh, what the hell!"

Beneath Leafy Canopies

Under leaves where shadows play,
The grape bunches joke all day.
"Got seeds?" one grape tries to tease,
"We're all just fruit with youthful fees!"

They giggle soft, in nature's draft,
Wishing they'd earn a hefty graft.
"Oh, did you hear the latest scoop?
That winery's holding a grape juice loop!"

Secrets of the Twisting Tendril

Tendrils twist with mischief bold,
Tickling grapes, making stories told.
"I've seen the sun, but never rain,
Lucky me, I'm more than just plain!"

They wrap around, a playful bind,
Always keeping grape minds aligned.
"Tell me your gossip, share your lore,
Let's toast to antics, oh and more!"

Shades of Fermented Dreams

In the dark of the barrel's hug,
The grapes hold dreams, a playful rug.
"Ferment us right, and we will dance,
With bubbles rising, we take a chance!"

Laughter echoes in the wine's embrace,
As grapes float in a fizzy race.
"To flavor, fun, and silly schemes,
Here's to life—and our wild dreams!"

Shadows in the Holder of the Fruit

Beneath the leafy hide, they schemed,
The fruits in chat with sunbeams gleamed.
"Why do we hang around all day?"
"It's comfy here, let's laugh and play!"

A cheeky berry cracked a joke,
The pears joined in, and laughter broke.
"What do we do when storms arrive?"
"We drink the dew... and stay alive!"

Garden of Hidden Delights

In this patch of green, the laughter grows,
With veggies plotting in their rows.
"Let's paint our leaves a brilliant red!"
"But what will happen to our bread?"

Tomatoes winked, with seeds of glee,
"A salad party? Count on me!"
Carrots grinned, both bold and brave,
"Let's host a feast! We'll dig our grave!"

Where the Grapes Gather Wise

Gathered round the barrel's side,
The grapes exchanged their tales with pride.
"Did you hear about that juicy bunch?"
"They say they'll ferment after lunch!"

One raisin groaned, "I'm feeling dry,"
"Perhaps it's time to swing and fly!"
"Let's find a vat where we can dive,"
"And sip our wine — oh, we'll survive!"

Touch of Autumn on the Vine's Embrace

As autumn hugs the garden tight,
The pumpkins laugh with sheer delight.
"We'll dress ourselves in straw and cheer!"
"Then spook the crows who come too near!"

The squash discussed their Halloween,
"Will we be carved? Or just be seen?"
They rolled together, side by side,
And planned a party, full of pride!

Threads of Vineyard Twilight

In the twilight glow, grapes start to dance,
They twirl and sway in a light-hearted prance.
The farmer chuckles, a humorous sight,
As he slips on a vine, what a comical flight!

Bottles like puppets, they wobble and roll,
Whispering secrets to the winemaker's soul.
Each cork a jokester, they pop with delight,
Making mischief until the moon is in sight.

The Embrace of Verdant Growth

Green leaves are giggling, under the sun,
Wishing for clouds to come join in the fun.
They tickle the grapes, who laugh in return,
In this leafy theater, the jokes take their turn.

The stout vines are tangled, a comedy scene,
Creating a maze that no one can glean.
"Where's the path?" shouts the neighbor, with glee,
"Just follow the laughter, it's as wild as can be!"

Echoes from the Orchard's Heart

Apples are gossiping, fresh off the tree,
Whispering tales of sweet jubilee.
"Did you hear what the berries told me?"
They burst into laughter, as happy as can be.

The branches start swinging, a whimsical crew,
As they share their stories, both old and new.
The orchard is vibrant, with joy wrapped in flair,
In the echoes of laughter, there's magic in the air.

Lush Comforts of Grape-Laden Boughs

Beneath the grape canopy, dreams softly rest,
Vines weave together, creating a nest.
The raccoon in pajamas, tipsy from wine,
Snores quietly, dreaming of grapes that entwine.

The breeze plays a tune, a symphonic touch,
While the grapes debate, "Do we taste too much?"
Each bubble of laughter, a sweet, bubbling cheer,
Under plush boughs where the jokes bloom sincere.

Echoes of Verdant Abundance

Beneath the leaves, the squirrels dance,
Chasing their tails in a wild romance.
Grapes giggle as they swing in the breeze,
Whispering secrets to the buzzing bees.

A plump tomato pulls a prank with flair,
Winking at pumpkins, who just can't compare.
The cucumbers chuckle in their leafy attire,
While the lettuce rolls over, caught in the mire.

Basking in the Gentle Shade

Bumblebees buzz with a wobbly flight,
Finding sweet treasures hidden from sight.
Carrots in rows hold gossip so grand,
While radishes play hide and seek in the sand.

Chili peppers throw a spicy soirée,
Dancing with greens in a carefree ballet.
The sunflowers gossip, tall and so proud,
As shadows stretch out, swirling like a cloud.

Guardian Spirits of the Garden

A garden gnome scratches his stone-cold head,
While mischievous rabbits steal lettuce instead.
The crows crack jokes with the chatty sky,
While ants march on, determined to try.

The wind whispers pranks to the flowers so bright,
Who sway and they giggle into the night.
The moon peeks in, with a mischievous grin,
While the frogs croak laughter, inviting you in.

Untold Stories Beneath the Canopy

Beneath leafy arches, the shadows do play,
As the mushrooms plot laughs at the end of the day.
A squirrel with secrets spins tales oh so tall,
While the thyme gives advice from the garden's great hall.

The peas form a chorus, all green and all sweet,
While the thyme gives advice, making gossip discreet.
The garden's alive with a vibrant routine,
Where plants, in their mischief, reign ever so keen.

A Canopy of Fruitful Dreams

Under a leafy green arch,
The grapes hang like little stars,
Whispering jokes to the breeze,
While squirrels practice their guitar.

A bee buzzes with a plan,
To throw a fruit party divine,
But underfoot, a hungry ant,
Scrambles for crumbs of wine.

A rabbit hops with flair,
Dancing like nobody's watching,
Stealing apples without a care,
While the trees are gossiping.

Oh, to lounge in this sweet shade,
Where laughter flows like nectar,
And the sun plays hide and seek,
In this daydream collector.

Secrets of the Leafy Realm

A chubby raccoon with a mask,
Hiding his snacks like a pro,
Tells tales of mischief so grand,
With a grape for a microphone, you know.

The leaves nod their green approval,
As critters dance a silly jig,
A frog croaks out a punchline,
While picking his nose with a twig.

A ladybug serves as DJ,
Spinning tunes on a daisy wheel,
Every bug takes to the floor,
In a dance-off that's quite surreal.

Amidst all the giggles and cheer,
Even shadows join in the fun,
As shadows twist and twirl,
'Neath the watchful eye of the sun.

Shadows Cast by Ripened Clusters

In a garden of jolly greens,
The fruits gossip, they can't keep still,
Melons roll and cherries tease,
Playing tag up the old windmill.

A zealous parsnip tries to sing,
But sounds like a quarrel of crows,
While carrots chuckle at his strife,
Sharing stories only they know.

The grapes laugh till they snort,
As grapes often do when they're ripe,
Creating shadows that dance on the ground,
As the veggies spin in a hype.

Oh, the joy of this festive feast,
Where silliness reigns supreme,
Each shadow casts its own rich tale,
In this orchard of dreams.

Under the Arched Foliage

Beneath the branches so wide,
A gathering of funny folks,
Tomatoes share wild bedtime stories,
While cucumbers crack up with jokes.

A snail with a top hat so grand,
Claims he's the king of this place,
He saunters slow with a flair,
While the radish rolls with grace.

The sun winks at playful shade,
As shadows dance upon the ground,
In a whimsical proving ground,
Where laughter knows no bounds.

As the day turns to slumber,
The leaves rustle soft goodbyes,
For tomorrow they'll cheerfully meet,
Under these fun-filled skies.

Enchanted Evening along the Rows

Beneath the stars, the grapes conspire,
They giggle softly, never tire.
A clumsy cat trips on the grass,
The neighbors watch, their laughter vast.

The moonlight dances on the fruit,
A raccoon steals some grapes—how cute!
He wears a mask, a bandit bold,
In nightly heists, his tales are told.

With every sip, a merry cheer,
The workers grin, no room for fear.
They raise a toast under the vines,
To laughter shared and earthy wines.

As twilight fades, the night unfolds,
With silly pranks in stories told.
The harvest moon winks with delight,
In the vineyard's charm, all feels just right.

Whispers in the Vineyard Mist

Through morning mist, the whispers tease,
Of grapes that giggle in the breeze.
A mouse in boots prances with glee,
While happy bees hum a melody.

A farmer's hat, all floppy and wide,
Flies off his head—oh, what a ride!
It lands on a scarecrow's nose,
Who chuckles at the farmer's woes.

The vines gossip in leafy shades,
While sneaky squirrels plan their raids.
A pressing question fills the air,
"Who will snatch the harvest fair?"

In the mist where laughter swirls,
The vineyard hosts its silly pearls.
With every tock, the clock will chime,
In this whimsy, all things feel sublime.

The Language of the Silent Harvest

The grapes are laughing, what a sight,
With whispers shared through day and night.
A jug of juice spills on the ground,
Making puddles where jokes abound.

The workers chat in playful tones,
While ducks parade on tiny thrones.
"Who spilled the wine?" the vines exclaim,
As they engage in grape-based games.

Each cluster beams with mischief's smile,
As shadows play and tricksters pile.
A hare hops past, so quick and spry,
Chasing the wind, oh my, oh my!

In secret corners, laughter brews,
With tales of mishaps, grape-sized news.
The harvest speaks in giggly ways,
As sunlight fades and twilight plays.

Secrets Among the Twisting Vines

Among the vines, a riddle weaves,
Where grapes share secrets, yes, it cleaves.
A hedgehog rolls by, don't make a fuss,
He's got the scoop—oh, who can trust?

The whispers slip through tendrils tight,
As butterflies flit in sheer delight.
"Who ate the grapes?" the vines demand,
While tipsy birds perform and stand.

When twilight drapes, the creatures jest,
Each twist and turn, a playful quest.
The scarecrow snores, his hat askew,
Dreaming of grapes, and a silly stew.

With each new dawn, the laughter swells,
In secret spots, the gossip dwells.
The vines, their antics, ever keen,
In this harvest haze, the laughter's seen.

Hideaway in the Grape Arbor

In the grape arbor, secrets hide,
With whispers of fruit, we share our pride.
Sipping on juice, feeling so spry,
Even the bugs seem to laugh and fly.

The sun peeks in, through leaves so bright,
Creating a drama, quite the delight.
Bees dance around, in swirling glee,
"Who drank my nectar?" whispers the tree.

Lucy the squirrel steals a grape or two,
While Benny the rabbit snoozes anew.
Laughter erupts, as birds take the stage,
We're all just actors, escaping our cage.

So let's toast to fun, under skies so clear,
In our merry hideaway, we've nothing to fear.
With each silly moment, our hearts come alive,
Together in mischief, we joyfully thrive.

The Silent Dance of Leaves

Leaves start to sway, like a dance in the breeze,
Beneath a grand arch, they sway with such ease.
A giggle erupts, from a close by vine,
"Ever tried to tango? Just give me a sign!"

Bobby the beetle joins in with flair,
His tiny feet tapping, without any care.
The wind plays the music, oh what a show,
Even the sunbeams can't help but glow.

Frogs leap in sync, with a splash and a croak,
They form quite a chorus, oh what a joke!
"Pass me a grape, while I cash in my rolls,"
The leaves giggle softly, hiding their goals.

So when in the grove, don't just stand still,
Join in the fun, embrace every thrill.
In the silent ballet, let spirits unwind,
For laughter and joy are the best you can find.

Under the Canopy of Time

Under the arch way, the past likes to play,
Timmy, the tortoise, is starting to sway.
"Just keep it slow, that's my life motto,"
As he winks at the breeze and takes a break, 'Oh!' he says,
'What a show!'

The grapes giggle down, they've seen it all,
From dances in spring to a summertime brawl.
"Last year's jam fight was quite a delight,"
As a bird regales all with tales of the night.

Tick-tock, the clock, hangs silent above,
While critters below are just full of love.
Under this shelter, no worries arise,
We keep all our secrets beneath leafy ties.

So raise up your glass, to moments divine,
With each silly story, let your heart shine.
For time is a trickster, with laughter it weaves,
In every sweet moment, our memory leaves.

Hushed Tales in the Vineyard

In the cool twilight, whispers awake,
The vineyard chuckles, "What mischief to make!"
With shadows at play, poured out like fine wine,
Gather 'round friends, let the fun intertwine.

The owls tell tales, of a grape throw contest,
Where tipsy raccoons were crowned as the best.
"Who knew?" said the fox, while munching his snack,
"I might shed a tear if they don't take it back!"

With each wrinkled leaf, a memory's told,
Of dancing and prancing, in vineyards of gold.
The night wears a cloak, stitched with delight,
As creatures convene, and the stars shine bright.

So step into dusk, where the laughter runs free,
In hushed tales and giggles, there's room for all three.
For under the stars, with stories that blend,
In the patchwork of night, we're all but good friends.

Beneath the Weight of Juicy Promises

Underneath the heavy bunch,
A squirrel dreams of grape for lunch.
With every twist, a tiny dance,
He nearly trips, oh what a chance.

The sunlight drips like sticky glue,
A picnic comes with buzzing crew.
The bugs are bold, they think they're guests,
While I just hope they skip the breasts.

A bottle rolls and gives a cheer,
As corks pop off, let's spread the cheer!
These grapes can't help but laugh and tease,
They'll never fit in trending cheese!

So here we lie in fruity dreams,
With juice that splashes, bursts, and beams.
I'm sticky now, but can't complain,
For all this laughter is not in vain.

Melodies of the Vine-Encased Hours

String beans strum like guitars fine,
While tomatoes waltz down the line.
We gather here, a fruit buffet,
As berries sway in sweet ballet.

The shadows hum a jazzy tune,
While fruits grow plump beneath the moon.
A watermelon sings with glee,
As bees join in a symphony!

With every squish, a giggle bursts,
The grapes confess of their sweet thirsts.
Here friends all stumble, slip, and slide,
A circus act, fruit's wacky ride!

So let's toast to this fruity spree,
To songs of joy and laughter free.
With every sip, we smile and cheer,
As jovial vines hold us so dear.

The Lure of Leafy Embers

Crisp leaves whisper secrets sly,
While squirrels giggle as they fly.
The sunbeams poke with playful beams,
A shadow's game of fruity dreams.

A carrot wears a leafy hat,
While radishes form a funny sprat.
They dance around, in soil they dig,
Just like real stars, quite the gig!

Even the roots join in the fun,
Poking at worms who want to run.
There's mischief brewing with each burst,
A garden plot that's always cursed!

Yet here we sit, our hearts will sing,
Among all greens, our love takes wing.
With giggles shared and wine so sweet,
Life's leafy games can't be beat.

A Tapestry Beneath the Grape Leaves

Beneath a drapery of greens,
Lay whispers of the best cuisines.
A salad bowl of laughs and dreams,
Where every vine and fruit redeems.

Cucumbers strut in fancy bowls,
With olives rolling on their strolls.
They jive and spin in tasty prance,
While radishes line up to dance!

Les grapes look on, oh what a sight,
As veggies party through the night.
They share their tales of juicy fame,
And all the while, they bubble lame.

At dusk, the laughter twirls and sways,
The fruits all shout, "Let's gift bouquets!"
With every crunch, a story beams,
In tangled vines, we weave our dreams.

A Veil of Verdant Hues

In a garden lush and wide,
Grapes conspire, jokes applied.
One claimed they'd run a race,
But tripped by their own grape face!

Old leaves whisper, full of glee,
Tales of how the beetles flee.
Beneath the vines, they play tag,
Oh, what an amusing rag!

Squirrels laugh, a cheeky bunch,
Trying hard to sneak a lunch.
Grapes retort with squishy cheer,
"Not this time, you furry dear!"

When twilight falls, the giggles bloom,
Wine glasses clink, they dance in gloom.
It's a party every night,
Underneath the leafy light!

Echoes of the Twining Roots

Twisted tales from roots so deep,
Wiggly plants in laughter leap.
"Hey, I sprouted first!" one said,
While another laughed, "You're misled!"

Tangled knots, oh what a sight,
Roots that argue who is right.
They wriggle like a silly worm,
Each one wishing for a turn.

Vines share puns in quiet tones,
Beneath the soil, they make their moans.
"Why did the grape grape?" it asked,
"To wine down, why are you masked?"

In the shade, a party grows,
Grapes in clusters, fun choreo.
They shake their leaves, a dance so grand,
Swaying together, hand in hand!

Lush Reflections in Twilight

In twilight's glow, the vines do jive,
With grapes who think they're so alive.
"Look at me! I'm really fine,"
Said one with sparkles on its vine!

The moonlight whispers silly tales,
Of dancing leaves and wine sales.
"Do we taste good?" one grape will shout,
"Or are we snacks the squirrels tout?"

Bees buzz around, a little sly,
"Join us now, don't be shy!"
Laughter ripples through the air,
As grapes and bees form quite the pair.

Twilight fades but not the fun,
Under this vine, we laugh and run.
Witty grapes and jolly bees,
Creating magic with the breeze!

Clusters of Forgotten Stories

In the hush of leafy dreams,
Grapes share tales of silly schemes.
"Remember when we rolled away?"
A burst of laughter in the hay!

Clusters gather, old and wise,
Trading secrets with twinkling eyes.
"I told a joke, it fell so flat,"
"But what's a flat grape? Just a mat!"

Beetles chuckle, sipping dew,
Thinking they're the funniest crew.
"Why did the vine go to the loo?"
"To witness all the grapes it grew!"

Under stars, the giggles grow,
In the vineyard, all's aglow.
With stories sweet, the night is bold,
In clusters, cabernet, and gold!

Nightfall in the Orchard

As daylight dims, the crickets sing,
An owl hoots loud, what joy they bring.
Beneath the trees, the shadows creep,
Let's not wake the bees, we'll just peep.

The plums are ripe, but oh so high,
A trampoline? Let's give it a try!
With a bounce and a twirl, we soar,
But land in a patch of soft, juicy gore.

The Cloak of Overhanging Vines

Those vines are thick, a perfect cloak,
But watch your head, it's no joke!
A tangle here, a shuffle there,
I'm stuck like glue, it's quite a scare!

The grapes dangle like shiny beads,
"Pick me first!" the cheeky fruit pleads.
But each one's a wriggly snack,
Who knew grapes could be such a whack?

Paths Woven in Green

We wander paths of tangled greens,
Where laughing squirrels plot their schemes.
A hidden trail leads to a prank,
With muddy shoes and a slippery flank.

"Step lightly now," I whispered low,
But then I tripped, oh what a show!
Down I go, it's quite a sight,
A mud-splattered giggle, oh what delight!

Fables of the Rustic Landscape

Once upon a time, in a field so grand,
Lived a cow with dreams that were quite unplanned.
"Let's dance by moonlight!" she would proclaim,
But all the other cows, well, thought it lame.

So she donned a tutu, not one to care,
And twirled in the night, with flair to spare.
The farmer laughed, the stars gave cheer,
A dancing cow? Now that's a frontier!

The Soft Breath of Summer's End

The grapes all giggle, what a sight,
Under the sun, they're feeling light.
They whisper secrets, oh so grand,
While the breeze gives them a gentle hand.

With every pluck, a joke unfolds,
Tales of the harvest, daring and bold.
They dance in the warmth, on the edge of cheer,
Summer's winks, oh how we near!

But as the nights start to whisper cool,
These jolly bunches feel quite the fool.
They laugh at the chill, "Is this a jest?
Or just the wind giving us a rest?"

So raise a glass, with a wink and a cheer,
To laughs in the field, each held so dear.
The end of the season, though bitter-sweet,
Leaves us with giggles, oh how we greet!

Hues of Hope in Grape-Swept Valleys

Painted in colors, bright and bold,
Tales of grapes, never getting old.
In valleys where laughter meets the sun,
Every bunch knows how to have fun.

Green and purple, swaying like dancers,
Even the bees join in the prancers.
They buzz and hum a very fine tune,
While the grapes chuckle under the moon.

"What's next?" they ask, with eyes all aglow,
"More picnics or parties? Let's steal the show!"
And with a bounce, they prepare to play,
Even the sunlight joins in the fray.

A rainbow of laughter, in every sip,
With jokes and puns, there's no chance to trip.
So here's to the fields of hope we find,
In grape-swept valleys, where joy is blind!

Fables from the Grapevine's Heart

Gather 'round, let's spin a yarn,
Of mischievous grapes and their charm.
They tell of dreams, not quite sincere,
"Can we turn to wine without a fear?"

Lurking nearby, the crows convey,
"Why is the grape always in dismay?"
A grape shouts back, "I'm just being wise!
You have no clue of our fun-filled lies!"

From juicy fables to festive tales,
Each one winds in the sun-drenched gales.
They weave their stories, with laughter loud,
Inviting all flora, under each cloud.

So when you sip that ruby red,
Remember the grapes and the words they said.
Life's a fable, a funny parade,
With every twist, a laugh is made!

Luminescence Among the Boughs

Glimmers of laughter light the way,
Through leafy tunnels where grapes play.
A sparkle here, a twinkle there,
Who knew the boughs could hold such flair?

As dusk creeps in, the jokes take flight,
Grapes reciting their limericks bright.
"Two grapes walked into a bar, you see,
One slipped and fell, now that's just silly!"

With every chuckle, the shadows sway,
Lighting the night in a playful display.
A soft glow rises, a party's delight,
Where even the darkness joins in the light.

So let's toast to this laughter we share,
Under the boughs that dance with flair.
In luminescence, we find our place,
With every giggle, there's joy to embrace!

Nestled in the Boughs' Serenity

In a treetop hideaway, laughter grows,
Squirrels debate on which nut to pose.
They've got a treehouse, it's quite the sight,
With acorns as snacks, they party all night.

With leaves all around, it's a lively scene,
Dancing around like they're on a screen.
"Who needs a floor?" calls out one in glee,
As they tumble down, just so carefree.

The sun above shines with a cheeky grin,
While birds join the fun, they're chirpin' in.
A festival of fluff, on branches so wide,
Where giggles echo and joy won't hide.

Nestled in branches, a joke takes flight,
"Why do trees never get lost at night?"
"Because they always know where the bark is near!"
And the laughter rises, full of good cheer!

Moonlight's Kiss on the Hidden Path

On a moonlit trail, the shadows take leads,
Bats in tuxedos fulfilling their needs.
Whispers of crickets serenade the night,
While frogs take the stage with leaps of delight.

A jovial owl hoots, "Who's there for a show?"
With fireflies twinkling like stars in a row.
"Join in the fun!" the forest invites,
As raccoons come dancing in comical tights.

The path twists and turns with glee and a wink,
Where starlit chuckles make shadows think.
Moonbeams are ready to twist and to shout,
As laughter rolls softly, no shadow of doubt.

"Why did the bat wing it on this route?"
"Because he heard it's where all pals boot about!"
And as the night hums a comical tune,
The path glimmers bright, 'neath the smile of the moon.

The Comfort of Grape-Heavy Dreams

In a vineyard vast, the dreams take flight,
Where grapes giggle softly, bathed in twilight.
They sway on the vine, all plump and round,
Sharing sweet jokes with the breeze all around.

"Why don't grapes ever get lost?" they jest,
"Because they follow the wine and it's always the best!"
With laughter like bubbles, they never feel shy,
Each grape a little joker under the sky.

As night settles in, with wishes so bright,
They sip on their dreams like they're sipping on light.
In a cozy embrace of the harvest so sweet,
Life's light-hearted moments unfurl at their feet.

Huddled together, they talk of the day,
With every soft giggle, they simply convey.
In this grape-heavy haven, they'll celebrate,
With jokes and warm wishes, they never wait!

Shadows Playing Along the Row

Along the rows where shadows play,
Are critters cracking wise in their charming display.
The vines wiggle in rhythm, a leafy dance,
While friends in the fields share a giggly chance.

"Why did the tomato blush?" asked a sprout,
"Because he saw the salad dressing, no doubt!"
Chortles erupt as the sun starts to dip,
In the garden of laughter, friendships equip.

The shadows stretch long, as daylight runs out,
Singing sweet tunes with a whimsical shout.
Chickens in hats strut with flair and delight,
As the garden joins in on this fanciful night.

With each little chuckle, the vines sway along,
Like a playful refrain to a silly old song.
And as the moon rises, the fun does not cease,
In this row of joy, they've discovered their peace.

Finding Solace Under the Foliage

Under the leaves, where laughter thrives,
I dance like a squirrel, doing high-fives.
The sun plays peek-a-boo, oh what a game,
With shadows that giggle and tease my name.

The branches sway, it seems they know,
The secret of joy, this leafy show.
I trip on roots, but that's just my flair,
In this green haven, I haven't a care.

A Palette of Green Beneath Our Feet

The grass wears green like a quirky hat,
Each blade a brushstroke, imagine that!
I paint my steps with whimsical hops,
As daisies murmur and the sunlight pops.

The earth is a canvas, squishy and bright,
I slip on my colors, oh what a sight!
With every footfall, laughter takes flight,
In this jolly green world, everything's right.

The Heartbeat of Unyielding Roots

In the ground below, a party's underway,
Roots twist and twirl like they're on display.
They gossip about the rain and the sun,
And chuckle together, oh what fun!

Beneath us, the soil hums a tune,
A melody played by the sun and the moon.
The roots stretch their arms, they jive and sway,
Making sure they enjoy every day.

Gaze into the Grape-Scented Dusk

As twilight descends with a giggly grin,
The vines whisper secrets, let the fun begin.
Grape juice drips from the tales they spin,
Tickling my senses, where to begin?

The stars pop out, like bubbles of cheer,
Lighting the dark with a twinkling sneer.
With silly conundrums, all wrapped in vines,
As laughter erupts like the best of wines.

Soft Serenades of the Cellar

Down below where the corkscrew twirls,
A mouse plays guitar as he twirls.
With a sip of wine, he strums away,
His tunes echoing in a jazzy fray.

Socks on feet, dancing on the floor,
The barrels sway, always wanting more.
As corks pop off, cheers fill the air,
While grapes gossip, a juicy affair.

Crickets chirp, in rhythm they sway,
Turning shadows into a play.
A chatter of bubbles, laughter and cheer,
In this cellar, there's nothing to fear.

So come join the fun, no need to act shy,
Raise your glass to the glowing sky.
For as long as the bottles keep smiling wide,
We'll party and laugh, side by side.

Dances of Light and Leaf

Sunlight filters through leaves so bright,
Dancing fairies twirl in the light.
A grape brigade rolls by with glee,
Making fruity jokes, it's a sight to see.

The older vines whisper, tales of old,
Of grapes that dared to be a little bold.
While squirrels tap dance on the old wood,
Snatching up snacks, as they should.

Bees buzz along, with their own little songs,
Their harmonies blend where the leaf throngs.
Laughter erupts from the apples nearby,
As the pears join in with a sonorous sigh.

In this vibrant space where silliness flows,
Life's the joke, and everyone knows.
So kick off your shoes, come join the play,
Where light and laughter brighten the day.

Breathing Beneath Canopies

Under the leaves where mischief brews,
A duck in shades prances, in funky shoes.
Sipping nectar, butterflies peek,
As the flowers gossip, causing a squeak.

Here comes a snail, with a shell so bright,
Sliding along, he's a funny sight.
He challenges a bug to a race so spry,
But loses, of course, as the beetles fly.

The sun winks down, casting shadows wide,
As watermelon seeds cheer from the side.
A picnic of dreams unfolds down below,
With laughter erupting as friendships grow.

The breeze carries giggles, whispers, and chats,
While the fruits throw a foam party with bats.
So come take a seat, enjoy the show,
In this leafy haven, let silliness flow.

Mellow Moods in Grape-Draped Bowers

In a cozy nook where the laughter glows,
Grapes wear crowns of fanciful bows.
A cat juggles berries, with a swish of his tail,
While the birds tweet riddles, without fail.

Below the arbors, shadows softly sway,
Dance-offs erupt, as friends come to play.
Munching on crackers, the giggles ignite,
As the sun dips low, painting all with light.

With every sip, stories unfold,
Of misadventures and moments bold.
The laughter wraps 'round like a favorite tune,
Each note echoing beneath the moon.

So lift your glass and smile wide,
In this grape-draped heaven, let joy reside.
For the world outside can wait in line,
While we share fun in this blend of wine.

Gazing Through the Grapes

Beneath the boughs we giggle and sigh,
Peering at grapes, we can't tell why.
A cluster of gossip, a berry of fun,
Who knew this hanging fruit could run?

We joke about wine stains on our shoes,
And pickle our thoughts like ancient brews.
With each juicy pop, we chuckle and cheer,
What tales will these grapes whisper this year?

Dancing around like clumsy fairies,
Watching the plant do its berry series.
We toast with our cups filled with fizzy air,
The bubbles spill secrets we gladly share.

So here's to the harvest, ripe and absurd,
The laughter and chaos can't be deterred.
In this fruity folly, we'll raise a toast,
To grapes that bring joy—the silliest boast!

Echoes of the Unseen Taster

In the vineyard's holler, who's sneaking a swig?
Could it be the ghost with a taste for the big?
Each swish of the glass tells a tale with a twist,
Of grapes that have vanished, they simply can't resist!

A phantom sommelier, he swirls and he peeks,
Leaving us guessing, it's all about leaks.
His laughter erupts like a cork in the air,
While we search for clues—oh, we're quite the pair!

Splashed with the juice of mishaps and glee,
He winks from the shadows, a ghost in the spree.
"Here's a hint," he chuckles, "just follow the stains,
For wine has a way of revealing your gains!"

So next time you sip on a bottle divine,
Remember the tales of the phantom nigh.
For laughter lies deep in each fruity delight,
With echoes of jest that linger each night!

Tracing the Veins of Life

Under the leaves where shadows play tricks,
We trace little paths with our fingers like sticks.
With a wink to the grapes, we sketch out a plan,
Pretending our lives are as grand as the span.

While dancing with clovers, we trip on the vine,
Each stumble a giggle, each fall a design.
Those veins woven thick tell the stories we crave,
Of sweet, tangy memories we're eager to save.

We swirl with the breezes, we dip and we dive,
A vine-filled adventure where laughter's alive.
We toast to our journeys, not just what we seek,
For the joy in the moments is far more unique.

So here's to our trails through the vine's playful maze,
With chuckles and heartbeats along every phase.
Let's raise up our glasses to grapey delight,
For tracing the veins brings us joy every night!

A Dance Beneath the Leafy Veil

Beneath leafy shadows, we whirl and we sway,
The grapes watch our shenanigans take center stage.
With twirls and capers, we send out a cheer,
"Let's drink to the follies that brought us right here!"

A grapevine's tango, we waltz through the rows,
With muddy old boots, we've got nowhere to go.
The leaves rustle softly as if they can laugh,
At our funny endeavors, a whimsical gaffe.

As we trip on the roots with tipsy delight,
The sun takes a bow, bidding farewell to night.
With giggles exploding, we give a high-five,
For dancing in vineyards keeps laughter alive.

So here's to the shadows that spark our delight,
Where the grapes have a view of our jolly night flight.
Under leafy umbrellas, we sway and we twirl,
A dance that's forever—come join in the whirl!

The Gathering of Twilight's Nectar

As night descends, we toast and cheer,
The grape juice flows, let's not show fear.
With glasses raised, our spirits gleam,
In this merry dance, we laugh and dream.

A squirrel steals snacks, so sly and quick,
We plot our schemes, and pick up sticks.
With every sip, our tales grow bold,
Of hidden treasures and legends told.

Dreams of Clusters and Leaves

We climb the trellis of whimsical thoughts,
Gathering gossip that life forgot.
The grapes whisper tales of crush and cheer,
Hoping our laughter rings in the ear.

Under the moon, we twirl and sway,
Sharing secrets we'll never relay.
With silly faces and wobbly stance,
We savor the moment, let's take a chance!

Beneath the Twisting Tendrils

Tendrils twist like our wildest plans,
A picnic blanket and cozy cans.
As the fireflies dance, we sip our brew,
And share our hopes, both old and new.

A raccoon sneaks through, what a sight!
Grabbing our fries in the pale moonlight.
We chuckle and giggle, it's quite absurd,
This gathering feels like our dreams unheard.

Whispers of the Grapevine

In shadows deep, where laughter hums,
We share our puns like little bums.
The grapes conspire, their message clear,
"Join in the fun, the night is near!"

With sticky fingers and fruity stains,
We dance like fools amidst the grains.
In whispered jokes and playful jeers,
We find our joy, dispelling fears.

In the Grove's Embrace

Under leafy blankets, we dance and sway,
While squirrels plot games, in their own quirky way.
Bees buzz with gossip, sipping nectar sweet,
While laughing at us, as we trip on our feet.

Sunlight filters down, like gold on the ground,
Each step feels like mischief, a joy newly found.
Crickets chirp laughter, they know all the tricks,
As we juggle our snacks, and dodge a few kicks.

With the breeze as our partner, we twist and spin,
In this merry frolic, let the fun begin.
We'll sip on our punch, with grapes as the treat,
And cheer to the shadows, where silliness meets.

When the day fades away, and shadows grow long,
We'll leave with a chuckle, our hearts like a song.
For nothing's more joyous than friends in the sun,
In the grove's warm embrace, we'll say it was fun.

Dappled Light on Distant Days

Beneath a tangled canopy, we frolic and play,
With dappled rays dancing, inviting our stay.
Every twist of the boughs makes a new, silly sound,
As we zip through the patch, oh what joy can be found!

Frogs leap over puddles, and here comes a chase,
While ants line the path, march in funny grace.
The sunlight joins in, tickling our noses,
With each giggle erupting, new laughter just grows.

Chasing after fireflies, we twirl in delight,
Making wishes on stars, that blink in the night.
Distant days become treasures, in our carefree spree,
As we giggle at shadows, that dance wild and free!

Yet soon we'll head home, with stories to share,
Of dappled days spent in the sun-kissed air.
In friendships well tended, our hearts will remain,
Woven close together, as sweet memories gain.

Solace Amongst the Vines

In a tangle of green, where the sun's rays peek,
A grape-scented paradise that hides little cheeks.
With each vine that we tumble, we shriek out our glee,
As chickens join in, with their own quirky spree.

Tiny critters gather, for laughter-filled feasts,
While we plan our next shenanigans, but wait, here comes yeast!
Let's not forget snacks, our true heart's intent,
With grapes on our fingers, our giggles unbent.

The vines wrap us snug, as the day gives a wink,
We can brew up a potion—if only we think!
But the only elixir, that flows from our chins,
Is the juice running down, from our grape-juice wins.

As twilight draws near, we count all our thrills,
With our hands full of snacks, and our hearts full of fills.
In a tangle of laughter, we'll echo this cheer,
For solace found here, is the reason we're near.

Beneath the Arched Boughs

Beneath arches of green, we find giggles galore,
As critters make plans, cracking jokes by the shore.
With laughter like music, we scamper and skip,
While ants hold a meeting, on the edge of our trip.

The shadows are playful, they dance in a line,
While we chase after tickles, in a bright sunlit shine.
Fluttering leaves rustle, with secrets to share,
As we dive into laughter, no worries or care.

We'll race with the breeze, as it pulls us away,
In this whimsical world, where the sun loves to play.
With our hearts as our compass, and joy as our guide,
We'll wander forever, like shadows side by side.

As daylight is fleeting, and the stars twinkle bright,
We'll gather our stories, with the moon as our light.
For under these boughs, with friends by our side,
We've found endless reasons, to laugh, dance, and glide.

In the Dappled Green Light

In a nook where the critters conspire,
A squirrel steals grapes, oh what a liar!
The sunlight winks through leaves high above,
While the bird squawks, "This is a setup, my love!"

A snail races past, or so he believes,
While rabbits hop by, wearing tiny sleeves.
Laughter erupts from the buzzing bees,
As ants march on, looking for cheese!

A frog slides in, with a plop and a splash,
"This party's for all, come join in the bash!"
But be careful, dear friend, watch your step tight,
Or you might just trip in the dappled green light.

So gather your friends, let the laughter unfold,
In this world of whimsy, watch the fun mold.
Nature's a stage, and we're in the play,
Where goofiness reigns, come out and sway!

Enchanted by Nature's Veil

Over yonder, a goat in a hat,
Trying to woo a plump little brat.
The trees giggle softly, swaying to the tune,
While a frog tunes his banjo under the moon.

The flowers gossip, petals all a-flutter,
"Have you seen this goat? His jokes make us mutter!"
But he's got charm, and he steals the show,
With jokes about cows and a dash of bravado.

A butterfly dances, spills juice from the fruit,
"Why did the grape stay in bed? Too tired to commute!"
Everyone chuckles, and the fun won't cease,
In this wild enchanted garden, we feel such peace.

Let's toast to the laughter, the silliness here,
With nectar so sweet, it wipes every tear.
For in every bloom and each leaf's sway,
Nature's hilarity turns night into day!

Beneath the Clusters' Glisten

Underneath vines where the sun likes to peek,
A rabbit complains, turning red with a squeak:
"I lost my lunch here, it rolled past the vine!"
Other critters join in, 'What's mine is all mine!'

A squirrel acts regal, laying claim to the scene,
His crown made of acorns: so silly, so keen!
They argue and bicker, then suddenly pause,
As a lizard shows up, proudly wearing his claws.

"What's all this fuss? Can't you guys just share?"
The lizard rolls his eyes, as he combs back his hair.
The laughter erupts, it's a party begun!
Beneath the grape clusters, we're all having fun!

So raise up your voices, let the giggles flow,
In this vine-wrapped world, we've got quite the show.
From bickers to laughter, joy's now the plan,
Let's eat up our troubles with some grape-loving man!

The Hidden Life Among the Roots

Down below where the mushrooms bicker,
A wise old tortoise takes a drink with a flicker.
The flowers debate, in their colorful chat,
"What's better than sunshine? A good old pratfall, that!"

A hedgehog walks by, his quills spiked with pride,
"I'm cooler than you, I'm nature's best guide!"
But the ants just keep marching, with no time to tweet,
Planning their heist of a picnic to eat.

The roots tickle toes of the folks passing near,
While rabbits do comedy, drawing quite a cheer.
They hop with such flair, wearing hats made of moss,
In this hidden life, being silly is boss!

So come take a stroll, let the humor ignite,
Beneath all the laughter, everything feels right.
For in this rich soil, where the fun never ends,
Discovery blooms and joy always blends!

A Canvas of Grape-Laden Serenity

Bunches of joy hang so low,
Underneath a sun-soaked glow.
The laughter spills like sweet, ripe wine,
Grapes giggle; say they're just fine.

With a clumsy squirrel prancing about,
Trying to steal what's clearly in doubt.
Each cluster winks, oh what a tease,
As tiny birds dance with the breeze.

Afternoons drift in a playful sway,
Where critters come out to frolic and play.
Boozy thoughts float in the air,
While shadows spin a whimsical affair.

Life's juiciness bursts at the seams,
With each sip flowing like silly dreams.
Under arboreal cover we sip,
In this riot of joy, we launch a trip.

Whimsy of the Ripe Harvest

The basket's full, oh what a sight,
A treasure of purple, pure delight.
Yet one grape rolls, with glee it goes,
A runaway gem, where mischief grows.

Grape vines whisper secrets so sweet,
Funny tales of lost little feet.
As the day drips, laughter's delight,
In the midst of a comical bite.

Each leaf giggles with a rustle,
While bees stumble in a drunken hustle.
Nature's funny show goes on,
As shadows dance with a cheerful yawn.

Everything ripe, all's perfectly true,
While squirrels plan a grand barbecue.
The laughter of harvest fills the space,
In this funny world, we all find grace.

The Stillness of Late Afternoon

As day yawns wide, the sun lazily beams,
Grapes cozy up, lost in sweet dreams.
Every leaf blowing, a gentle cheer,
While critters plot what they hold dear.

Time stands still, then suddenly slips,
Like juice that dribbles from happy lips.
Silly shadows start to sway,
Inviting whispers to dance and play.

The bottle cap pops with a jolly sound,
As giggles chase the breeze around.
Every ounce of laughter spills,
Painting joy on all the hills.

In silence, the funny stories brew,
Of wobbly vines and skies so blue.
Step back, enjoy this curious view,
In afternoon's stillness, life feels new.

Drunken Fantasies in the Lenient Breezes

Breezes soft, with tales untold,
Grapes spill secrets, bold yet old.
As we sip and sway in the light,
Funny dreams take playful flight.

A cork pops off with a joyful cheer,
As whispers bring the critters near.
Every sip swirls with a twist,
Laughing so hard, we can't resist.

Late-day antics like wobbly vines,
Crafting stories in drunken lines.
With each chuckle underneath the moon,
Grapes become stars; we sway to the tune.

Laughter floats on the dill breeze,
Sharing a table with honey bees.
Drunken fantasies fill the air,
With giggles that follow us everywhere.

www.ingramcontent.com/pod-product-compliance
Lightning Source LLC
Chambersburg PA
CBHW072141200426
43209CB00051B/236